SOUND PATTERNS

Sequential Sight-Reading in the Choral Classroom

Book 1

BY EMILY CROCKER

Available Separately
SOUND PATTERNS
Sequential Sight-Reading in the Choral Classroom

Teacher Edition (00324672)
(Includes My Library access to digital notation and audio files)

Classroom Bundle (00324673)
(Includes Teacher Edition and 30 Student Editions)

ISBN 978-1-5400-7271-9

Visit Hal Leonard Online at
www.halleonard.com

Contact us:
Hal Leonard
7777 West Bluemound Road
Milwaukee, WI 53213
Email: info@halleonard.com

In Europe, contact:
Hal Leonard Europe Limited
42 Wigmore Street
Marylebone, London, W1U 2RN
Email: info@halleonardeurope.com

In Australia, contact:
Hal Leonard Australia Pty. Ltd.
4 Lentara Court
Cheltenham, Victoria, 3192 Australia
Email: info@halleonard.com.au

TABLE OF CONTENTS

ABOUT THE AUTHOR

EMILY HOLT CROCKER taught public school music at all levels for 15 years in Texas. In 1989, she joined Hal Leonard, the world's largest publisher of choral and classroom publications, becoming Vice President of Choral Publications in 2000, and retiring in 2017 after 28 years with the company. In 1994 she founded the Milwaukee Children's Choir and was artistic director of the group until 2009 and in 2019 named Director Emeritus. In 2009 she founded the Vocal Arts Academy of Milwaukee, leading that group until 2015.

As a composer, Ms. Crocker's works have been performed around the world, and she has received ASCAP awards for concert music since 1986. She is well known for her work in developing choral instructional materials, including the choral textbook series *Essential Elements for Choir* (1995), *Experiencing Choral Music* (2005), and *Voices in Concert* (2016). She received the Distinguished Citizen Award – Professional in the Arts in 2009 from the Civic Music Association of Milwaukee and was named Honored Alumna for 2009 by the University of North Texas College of Music. In 2017 she received the Outstanding Service Award from the Texas Choral Directors Association, and in 2019 she was inducted into the Fort Worth Independent School District Wall of Fame.

INTRODUCTION

by Emily Crocker

Sound Patterns has been created to introduce beginning sight-readers to basic notation and music literacy through the overall context of melodic patterns within measures and phrases, so that the student will quickly comprehend those concepts while finding it easy and fun. The terminology used is accurate, but memorizing these terms is less important than the motivation of reading "real music," complete with lyrics, dynamics and accompaniment, along with preparatory exercises that are interesting and authentic. The melodies in these exercises are based on the "sound patterns" that form the basis of traditional Western music. The exercises may be sung in unison or combined with other exercises on the same page, creating opportunities for variety and the repetition needed to internalize the concepts being practiced.

This book focuses on three keys: C, F and G major, basic rhythms, and simple intervals in the tonic, dominant and subdominant chords. Students will immerse themselves in these tonalities, allowing enough practice to become sufficiently familiar with the basics before moving on to a new concept. After moving through the keys of C, F and G, future volumes in this series will expand to offer additional keys and modes.

Sound Patterns may be used with beginners of any age, and is ideal for students in late elementary and middle school. Teachers are encouraged to include material from **Sound Patterns** in every rehearsal. The goal is not to "finish the book" but to absorb the concepts. Take time to repeat exercises, combine lines in different ways, play games and find creative ways to repeat and polish songs, so students become fluent in all the skills needed to become literate musicians and sight-readers. As these skills are practiced, students will become more confident and eager to build their musical skills, as they are building a musical lexicon that will form the basis of their music literacy. The Teacher Edition (HL00324672) offers teaching suggestions and My Library online access to digital notation and audio files.

Sound Patterns updates and streamlines the concepts originally presented in the series **Patterns of Sound**, written over thirty years ago with Joyce Eilers, but all exercises and songs in this book have been newly composed, the terminology updated and the learning sequence revised.

As a companion resource, I recommend **Making Sight-Reading Fun!** by Mary Jane Phillips. It includes 20 creative games and activities to motivate elementary and middle school students along with other useful tips and techniques for teachers.

MAKING SIGHT-READING FUN!
Choral Games for Students and Teachers
by Mary Jane Phillips
Hal Leonard 00153841

CHAPTER 1
BEAT & RHYTHM

GIVE US THE BEAT

Beat

Beat is a steady recurring pulse. Each one of these vertical lines represents one beat. Practice keeping a steady beat. Clap, tap or chant with a clock or metronome.

| | | | | | | | | | | | | | | | |

Note Values

In music, a **note** represents musical sound. The duration of the sound (or how long the note is held) is represented by different note values. Three common note values include:

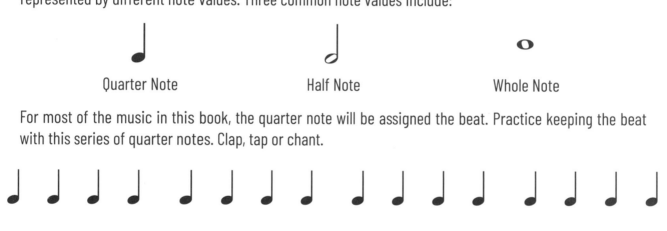

Quarter Note   Half Note   Whole Note

For most of the music in this book, the quarter note will be assigned the beat. Practice keeping the beat with this series of quarter notes. Clap, tap or chant.

The chart below represents four beats of sound with four quarter notes having the same duration as two half notes or one whole whole note.

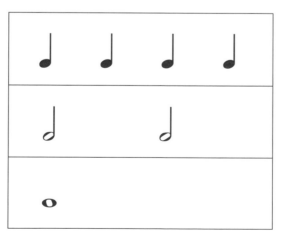

The speed of the beat, faster or slower, is called **tempo**.

RHYTHM MIX-UP

Rhythm is the organization of sound duration (length). Notes can be combined into different patterns to create rhythm. Clap, tap or chant each line.

Clap, tap or chant each line. Repeat as needed for confidence and accuracy. Divide into groups and combine lines. Be sure to keep a steady beat.

MEASURE, METER AND BARLINE

Each of the boxes below includes four beats.

Another way to organize rhythm is with barlines and measures. A **barline** is a vertical line that separates rhythm patterns into smaller sections called **measures**.

A **double barline** indicates the end of a section or piece of music.

Meter is a form of rhythm organization. The numbers that identify the meter are called the **time signature** and are placed at the beginning of a song or section of a song.

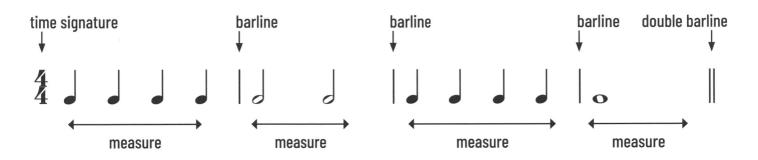

Here are three common time signatures:

$\frac{4}{4}$ = four beats per measure
= quarter note receives the beat

$\frac{3}{4}$ = three beats per measure
= quarter note receives the beat

$\frac{2}{4}$ = two beats per measure
= quarter note receives the beat

RHYTHM MIX-UP

Identify the meter and clap, tap or chant each line.

ANIMALIA
Speech Chorus

Apply what you've learned about music reading to this short speech chorus. After you sight-read the rhythm, repeat with the printed text and *dynamics* to add interest.

Musical Terms

dynamic – a marking which indicates the loudness or softness of the music

p - piano (soft)

f - forte (loud)

- crescendo (gradually louder)

- decrescendo (gradually softer)

Words and Music by
EMILY CROCKER

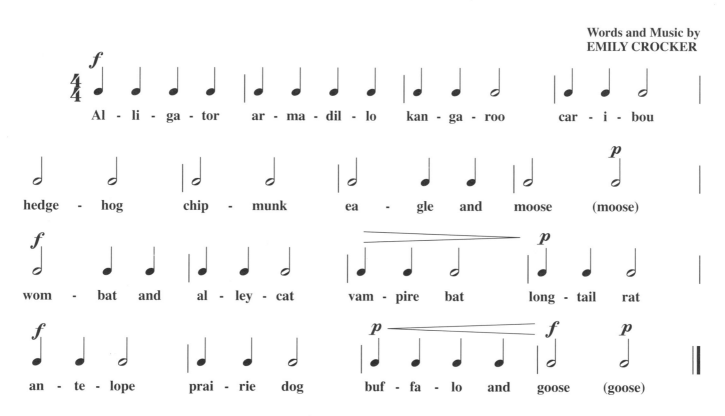

CHAPTER 2
STAFF, SCALE & PITCH

Pitch refers to the highness or lowness of musical sound. Music **notes** are another name for pitch. Music notes are identified by the first seven letters of the alphabet, from A to G.

The piano keyboard is organized by groups of two and three black keys. The white key to the left of a group of two black keys is always C. The C nearest the middle of the keyboard is called **Middle C**.

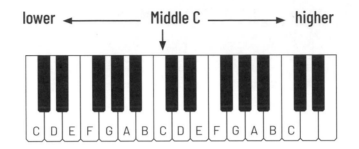

A **staff** is a graph of 5 lines and 4 spaces on which music is written. The lines and spaces are numbered from the bottom up, so the bottom line is line 1 and the bottom space is space 1. The symbol at the beginning of the staff on the left side is called a **treble clef**. It is sometimes called the G clef because the curve of the clef loops around the G line.

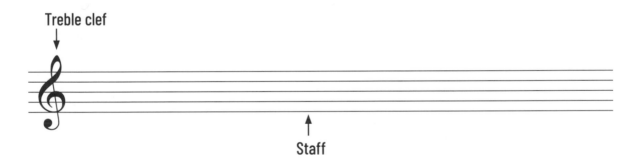

Middle C has its own little line below the treble staff. This is called a **ledger line**. Ledger lines can be used below or above a staff.

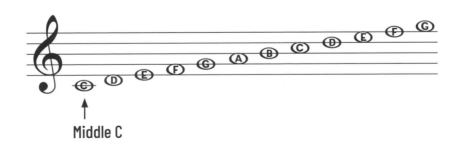

SCALE AND PITCH NAMES

A **scale** is a succession of pitches higher and lower. The word comes from the Italian word *scala* which means "ladder."

Play a scale on a keyboard starting on C and ending on C, using only the white keys and without skipping any keys. This forms a pattern of pitches called a **major scale**.

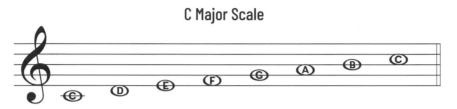

C Major Scale

Another way to name pitches is by using **solfège**, a method for singing melodies using Latin note names. Sing the C major scale using solfège.

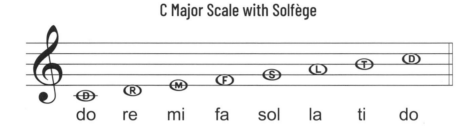

C Major Scale with Solfège

do   re   mi   fa   sol   la   ti   do

Read or echo-sing these pitch patterns in solfège.

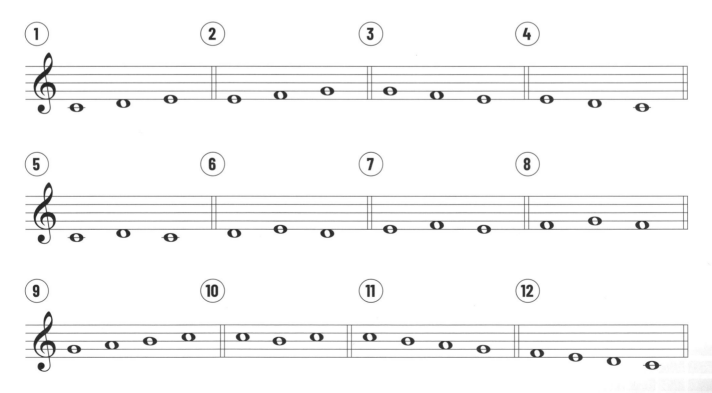

MELODY MIX-UP

These exercises combine rhythm and pitch to produce **melody**. Read and chant the rhythm first, then add pitch. Each exercise extends to the double barline. When you are successful in singing these exercises, you may sing the lines in any combination to produce **harmony**, two or more pitches sounded simultaneously.

FAR ACROSS THE VALLEY

For Unison Voices and Piano

Words and Music by
EMILY CROCKER

Far a-cross the val-ley a voice is call-ing me. It ech-oes in the twi-light and whis-pers through the trees.

CHAPTER 3
RESTS

RESTS

A *rest* is silence in music. Rests come in a variety of durations, just like notes. These silences are just as important as the notes. Rests and notes of the same name share the same duration. The beat continues, no matter what type of note value or rest is used.

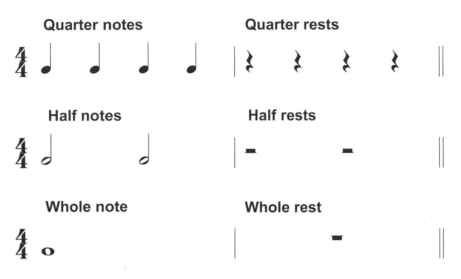

Speak, tap or clap these rhythm exercises separately or in any combination.

PANCAKES!

Speech Chorus

Words and Music by
EMILY CROCKER

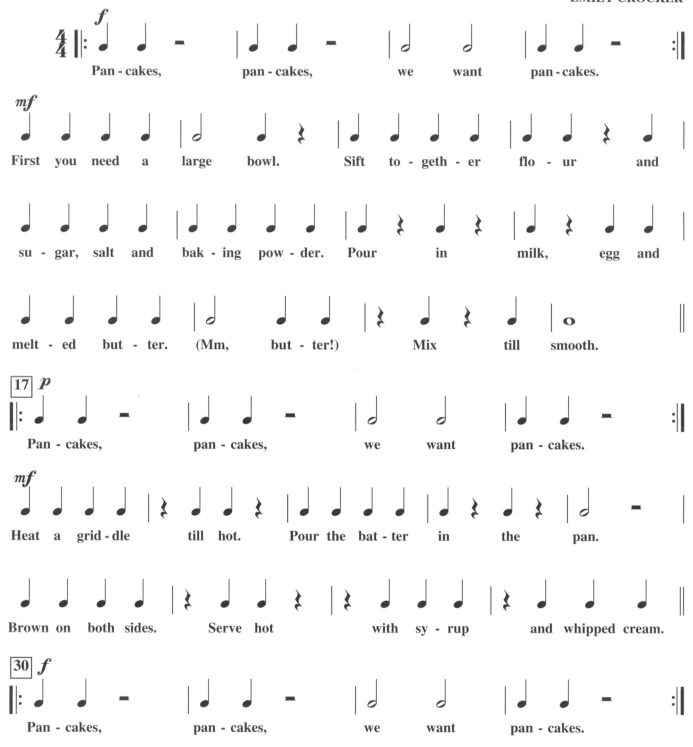

MELODY MIX-UP

Rests

Sight-read and practice these melody exercises with rests. Any exercise may be sung in unison or in combination with any other.

MELODY MIX-UP

More Practice with Notes and Rests

Sight-read and practice these melodic exercises with rests. Any exercise may be sung in unison or in combination with any other.

MATCH CATS ON THE AVENUE

For Unison Voices and Piano

Words and Music by
EMILY CROCKER

Match Cats stroll-ing down the av - e - nue.

Cool Cats just look-ing for some-thing to do.

In a haze, in a daze,

cra - zy, la - zy, what now to do?

Match Cats stroll - ing down the av - e - nue.

Cool Cats just look - ing for some - thing

to do. Match Cats! Cool Cats!

CHAPTER 4
INTERVALS, TONIC CHORD

INTERVALS

REVIEW: A *scale* is a succession of pitches higher and lower. The C major scale is a specific order of pitches which starts and ends on C. C is the **tonic**, also known as the *home tone* or *keynote*. The tonic is identified by the Roman numeral I.

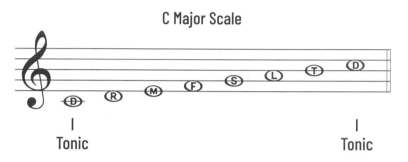

The distance between any two notes is called an **interval**. Melodies can move by **steps**, or from one pitch to next pitch higher or lower. Melodies can also move by **skips** – intervals greater than a step.

Here are some common intervals in the key of C.

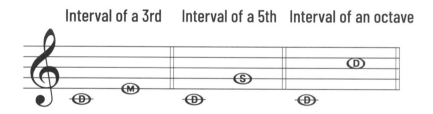

Sight-read or echo-sing these interval exercises in the key of C.

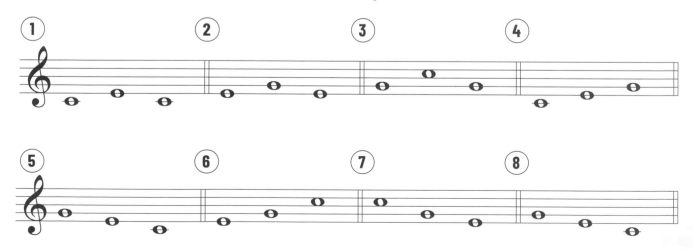

TONIC CHORD

A *chord* is the combination of three or more tones played or sung simultaneously.

Chord examples

A *triad* is a special type of three-note chord over a root tone. When a triad is built on the keynote of a major scale, it is called the *tonic chord*.

C Major Tonic Chord

Sight-read or echo-sing these melody patterns which use the tonic chord.

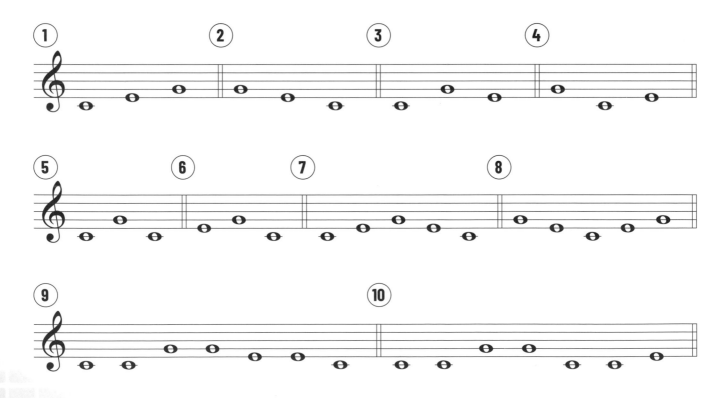

MELODY MIX-UP

Steps and Skips

Practice reading and singing music which has both steps and skips. Sing the scale and chord to establish the tonality, then sing the exercises separately and then in any combination.

C Major Scale

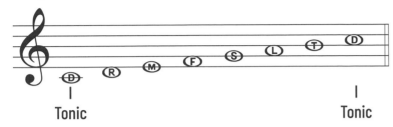

Tonic   Tonic

C Major Tonic Chord

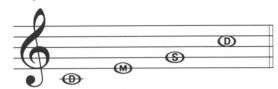

COFFEE

For Unison Voices, Piano and Percussion

Words and Music by
EMILY CROCKER

Light Calypso (♩ = ca. 128)

Lyrics (m. 9): Cof - fee, she loves her cof - fee. Just pour the

20

CHAPTER 5

F MAJOR

A NEW KEY

F Major

REVIEW: A C major scale is a specific order of pitches which starts and ends on C. Major scales can be built on other keys as well.

The **F major scale** starts and ends on F. To play a major scale starting on F, you will need to play a **B-flat** to create the specific order of pitches in a major scale.

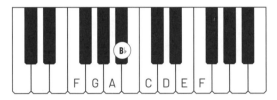

A **flat** is a symbol that means a pitch is to be lowered to the next lower pitch. Therefore, a flat to the left of the pitch B means you should play or sing the next lower pitch, B-flat.

B-flat

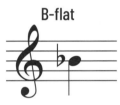

Another way to indicate B-flat is to be played is to put a flat on the B line to the right of the clef sign. This is called a **key signature** and means that all the B notes in the music are to be played as B-flat.

B-flat in the key signature

Sing or play the F major scale written on the staff:

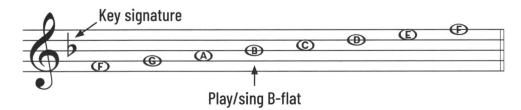

F MAJOR PRACTICE

Music can be written in many different keys and sometimes not in any key at all. With practice, a musician learns to sight-read and perform music in any key. As you sing these exercises, F now becomes the keynote, or **do.** The scale patterns shift to the new key.

F Major Scale

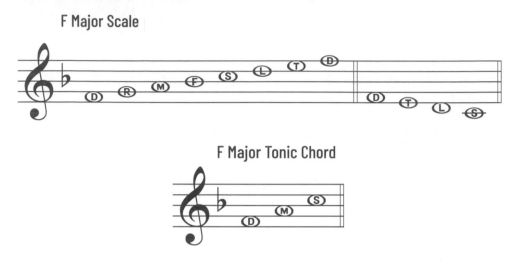

Identify the solfège, echo sing and read these melody patterns in the key of F.

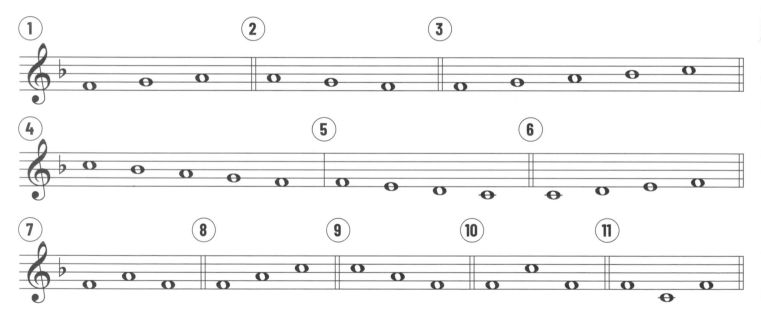

MELODY MIX-UP

F Major Practice

Using the F major scale and chord patterns as a guide, sight-sing these F major exercises.

METER IN THREE

F Major

REVIEW: *Meter* is a form of rhythm organization. The numbers that identify the meter are called the *time signature* and are placed at the beginning of a song or section of a song.

$\mathbf{3}$ = three beats per measure
$\mathbf{4}$ = quarter note receives the beat

In a meter of 3/4, a ***dotted half note*** is held for three beats. The dot extends the duration of the note by half its value. Therefore, a dotted half note lasts as long as a half note plus a quarter note: *3 beats.*

is equivalent in duration to

These exercises include the dotted half note. Sight-read and practice each line separately and in any combination.

SOARING, GLIDING

For Unison/Opt. 2-Part Voices and Piano

Words and Music by
EMILY CROCKER

Part I: Like an ea-gle fly-ing so high o-ver mead-ow and down to the sea. Soar-ing, glid-ing, my spir-it is free,

Part II (opt.): Like an ea-gle fly-ing so high o-ver mead-ow and down to the sea. Soar-ing, glid-ing, my spir-it is free,

seek-ing to find my own des - ti - ny. Soar - ing,

seek-ing to find my own des - ti - ny. Soar - ing, glid - ing,

glid - ing,

soar - ing, glid - ing,

seek-ing to find my own des - ti - ny.

seek-ing to find my own des - ti - ny.

CHAPTER 6
EIGHTH NOTES

REVIEW: The **_beat_** is a steady recurring pulse. **_Rhythm_** is the organization of sound duration. Notes can be combined into different patterns to create rhythm. The **quarter**, **half** and **whole** note represent different lengths or duration of sound:

An **_eighth note_** is half the duration of a quarter note. Two eighth notes have the same duration as one quarter note.

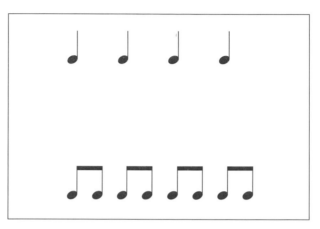

Clap, tap or chant these rhythm exercises that use eighth notes. Repeat as needed for confidence and accuracy.

RHYTHM MIX-UP

Eighth Note Practice

Identify the meter, then sight-read and practice these eighth note exercises. Combine lines that are in the same meter. Clap, tap or chant.

CREEPY CRAWLY CREATURES

For Unison/Opt. 2-part Voices and Piano

Words and Music by
EMILY CROCKER

Funky (♩ = ca. 124)

Piano

Part I

Bats in the bel - fry,   bugs in the base - ment,

Part II (opt.)

Bats in the bel - fry,   bugs in the base - ment,

rab-bits in the flow-er-beds,   mice in the pan - try,

rab-bits in the flow-er-beds,   mice in the pan - try,

squirrels in the at - tic, squirrels in the at - tic.

squirrels in the at - tic, squirrels in the at - tic.

19 Rats in the cel - lar,

Rats in the cel - lar,

snakes in the tall grass, spi - ders in the spice drawer,

snakes in the tall grass,

CHAPTER 7
DOMINANT CHORD

DOMINANT CHORD

REVIEW: The *tonic chord* is a chord built on the home tone (keynote) of the scale: *do mi sol*.

F Major Tonic Chord

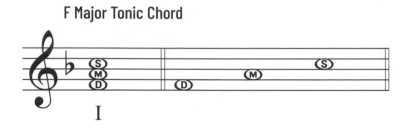

Chords can be built on any note of the scale. The *dominant chord* is a chord built on the fifth note of a scale, using the pitches *sol ti re*. The dominant is identified by the Roman numeral V.

Dominant Chord

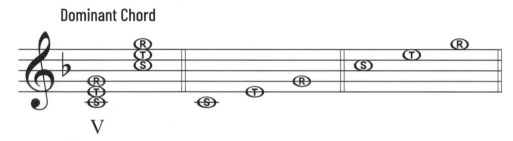

Echo-sing and sight-read these melody patterns that include intervals from the tonic and dominant chords in F major.

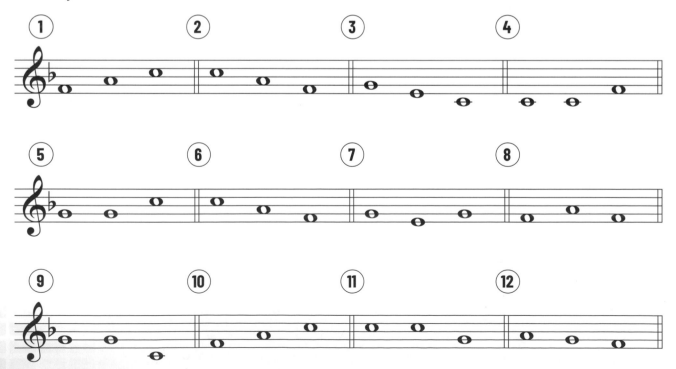

MELODY MIX-UP

Tonic and Dominant Intervals

Practice sight-reading and singing music which has intervals from both the **tonic** and **dominant** chords in F major. Each exercise may be combined with any other exercise on this page.

MELODY MIX-UP

3/4 Meter

Practice sight-reading and singing music with tonic and dominant chord intervals. Notice that some exercises do not begin on **do**. Establish the tonality by singing the scale, then find the starting pitch. Each exercise may be combined with any other exercise on this page.

MORE ABOUT EIGHTH NOTES

REVIEW: An eighth note is half the duration of a quarter note. Two eighth notes have the same duration as one quarter note.

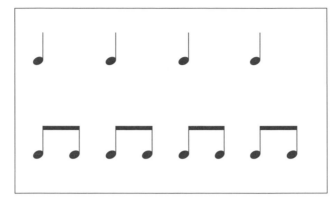

The eighth note has a corresponding rest, the ***eighth rest*** which has the same duration as an eighth note.

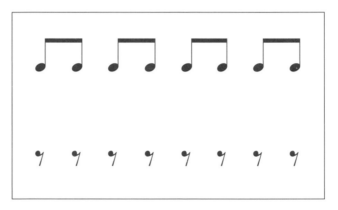

Eighth notes may be notated singly, with a ***stem*** and a ***flag***. The stem may go up or down, depending where the note appears on the staff. Eighth notes may also be grouped together by a ***beam***.

RHYTHM MIX-UP

Eighth Notes and Rests

Sight-read and practice these rhythms with precision. Use a metronome and experiment with different tempos, concentrating on keeping the beat and division steady.

BIP BOP

Speech Chorus

Words and Music by
EMILY CROCKER

MELODY MIX-UP

More Eighth Notes and Rests

Practice sight-reading and singing music which includes eighth notes and rests. Notice that not all exercises start on *do*.

MORE ABOUT CHORDS

REVIEW: The ***tonic chord*** is a chord built on the home tone (keynote) of the scale: ***do mi sol***. The ***dominant chord*** is a chord built on the fifth note of the scale ***sol ti re***. Practice this chord exercise to gain accuracy and confidence singing these intervals.

I (Tonic)   V (Dominant)   I   V   I

The ***dominant*** chord often includes an added pitch, ***fa*** (the 4th note of the scale), making this the ***dominant seventh*** chord, because ***fa*** is seven pitches higher than ***sol***. Practice these exercises to hear and learn the sound of this added tone in the dominant chord.

Dominant 7th Chord

I   V7   I   V7   I

Practice building three and four part chords. Divide into groups with each group singing one of the chord tones. Listen to each other and tune the chord.

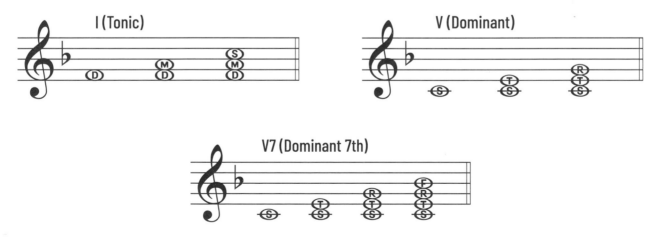

I (Tonic)   V (Dominant)

V7 (Dominant 7th)

MELODY MIX-UP

Interval Practice

Practice sight-reading and singing music which includes intervals in the *tonic* and *dominant 7th* chords. Notice that not all exercises start on *do*.

THE KING'S THREE SONS

For Unison/Opt. 2-Part Voices and Piano

Traditional English
Arranged with New Lyrics by
EMILY CROCKER

CHAPTER 8

G MAJOR, PICK-UPS, SLURS, TIES

A NEW KEY

G MAJOR

REVIEW: A C major scale is a specific order of pitches which starts and ends on C. The F major scale starts and ends on F and includes a B-flat.

The **G major scale** starts and ends on G. To play a major scale starting on G, you will need to play an **F-sharp** to create the specific order of pitches in a major scale.

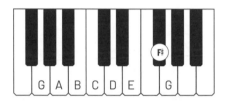

A **sharp** is a symbol that means a pitch is to be raised to the next higher pitch. Therefore, a sharp to the left of the pitch F means you should play or sing the next higher pitch, F-sharp.

F-sharp

Another way to indicate F-sharp is to be played is to put a sharp on the F line to the right of the clef sign. This is called a **key signature** and means that all the F notes in the music are to be played as F-sharp.

F-sharp in the key signature

Sing or play the G major scale written on the staff:

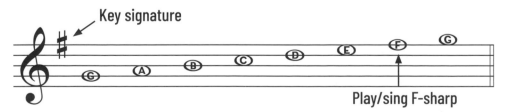

G MAJOR PRACTICE

Music can be written in many different keys and sometimes not in any key at all. With practice, a musician learns to sight-read and perform music in any key. As you sing these exercises, G now becomes the keynote, or **do.** The scale patterns shift to the new key.

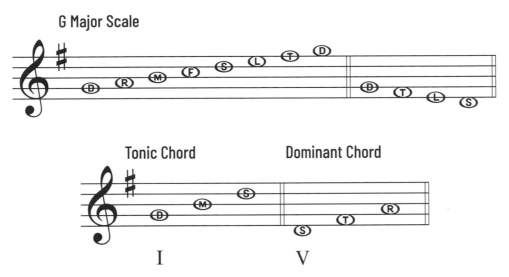

G Major Scale

Tonic Chord   Dominant Chord

I   V

Identify the solfège, echo sing and read these melody patterns in the key of G.

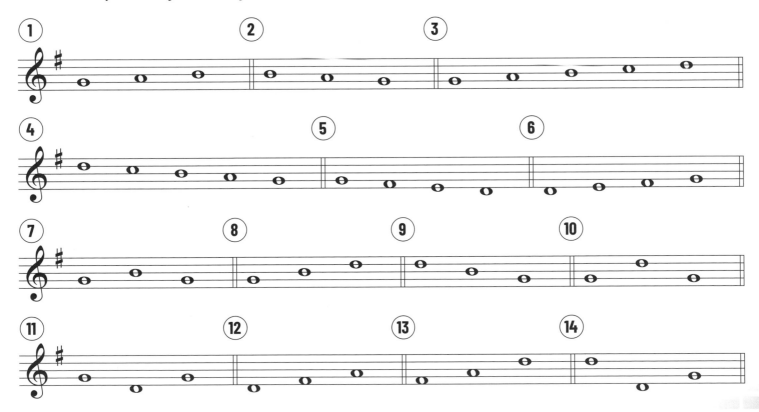

MELODY MIX-UP

G Major Practice

Practice sight-reading and singing music in the key of G. Notice that not all exercises start on **do**. Sing each exercise separately and in combination with others.

MORE ABOUT RHYTHM

Pick-ups and Slurs

A **pick-up** is one or more notes which occur before the first barline. Other names for **pick-up** are **upbeat** or **anacrusis**.

A **slur** is a curved line that connects two or more pitches that are to be played or sung **legato** (smoothly) on a single word or syllable.

Sing this traditional song that uses both a pick-up and slurs.

WASSAIL, WASSAIL

Traditional English
Lyrics adapted by EMILY CROCKER

MORE ABOUT RHYTHM

Ties

A **slur** is a curved line that connects two or more pitches that are to be played or sung legato (smoothly) on a single word or syllable.

A **tie** is a curved line that connects two notes of the same pitch to extend the duration (length) of the sound. The first note is played or sung and held through the entire second note.

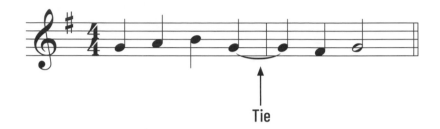

Tie

Practice reading these examples below.

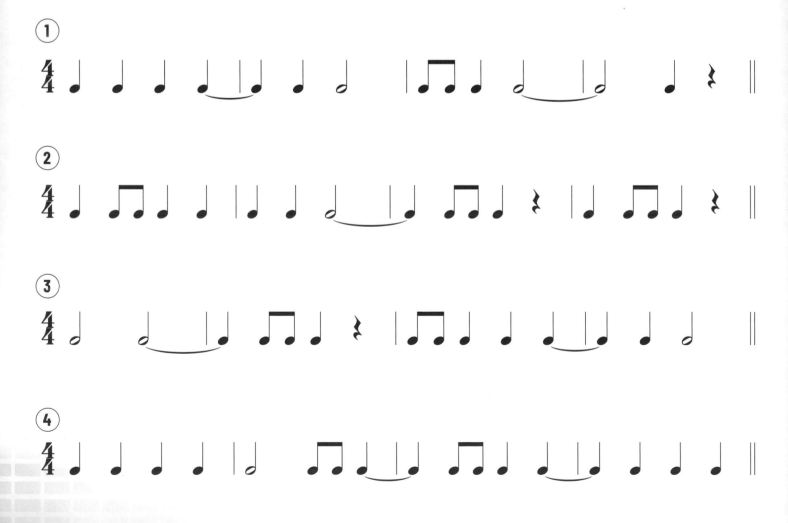

MELODY MIX-UP

Pick-ups and Ties

Practice sight-reading and singing music in the key of G. Notice the pick-ups and tied notes. Sing each exercise separately and in combination with others.

WASSAIL, WASSAIL

For 2-Part Voices, Piano and Drum

Traditional English
Arranged with Additional Lyrics by
EMILY CROCKER

door. "Bring the Was - sail___ down or we'll sing some more!"

door. "Bring the Was - sail___ down or we'll sing some more!"

Play

12

22

Was - sail, Was - sail,___ all

Was - sail, Was - sail,_____

18

o - ver the town!___ The wind it is cold with the snow___ fall - ing

_____ The wind it is cold._____

24

CHAPTER 9
SUBDOMINANT CHORD

SUBDOMINANT CHORD

REVIEW: The **tonic chord** is a chord built on the home tone (keynote) of the scale: **do mi sol**. The **dominant chord** is a chord built on the fifth note of a scale, using the pitches **sol ti re**.

Tonic Chord
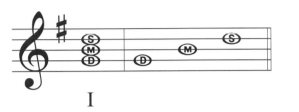
I

Dominant Chord
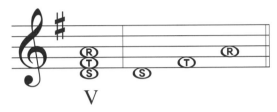
V

Chords can be built on any note of the scale. The **subdominant chord** is a chord built on the fourth note of a scale, using the pitches **fa la do**. The subdominant is identified by the Roman numeral IV.

Subdominant Chord
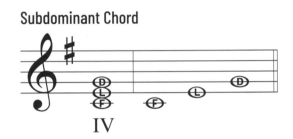
IV

Echo-sing and sight-read these melody patterns that include intervals from the tonic, dominant and subdominant chords in G major.

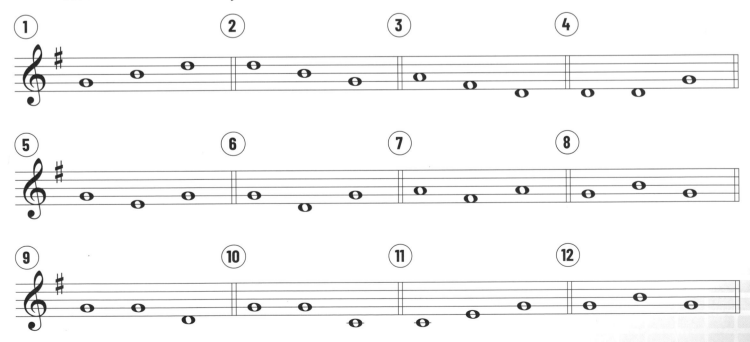

MELODY MIX-UP

Key of G Practice

Practice sight-reading and singing music in the key of G. Identify the meter and notice the intervals from the tonic, dominant and subdominant chords. Sing each exercise separately and in combination with others.

MELODY MIX-UP

Key of G Practice

Practice sight-reading and singing music in the key of G. Identify the meter and notice the intervals from the tonic, dominant and subdominant chords. Sing each exercise separately and in combination with others.

STARSHINE, MOONLIGHT

For 2-Part Voices and Piano

Words and Music by
EMILY CROCKER